Moving Through Trauma Into Transformation

A Family Law Perspective

Steve Shapiro, Esq.

Jacobs & Whitehall
21750 Hardy Oak Blvd
Suite 104
#51700
San Antonio, Texas 78258
www.jacobsandwhitehall.com

Ordering Information:

Quantity sales. Special discounts are available on quantity purchases by corporations, associations, and others. For details, contact the publisher at the address above.

Orders by U.S. trade bookstores and wholesalers. Please contact Jacobs & Whitehall: Tel: (888) 991-2766 or visit www.jacobsandwhitehall.com.

Printed in the United States of America

Published in 2022

PREFACE

This book is written as a primer for anyone who is experiencing difficult family separation, or breakup, or is aware that something catastrophic might be occurring in their family system. We have all experienced broken relationships in our lives. My hope in writing this primer is that you can gain some wisdom and perspective that guides your approach moving forward, within the legal framework, or some other creative outcome that can restore a fully functioning family system.

Family law is a multi-disciplined process or system requiring the best practices in psychology, financial planning, and developing legal structures that work for the entire family. Collaborative Law practice is one such example that brings a humane and compassionate approach to a family breakup and uses this foundation to find sustainable and durable solutions towards resolving a dispute. As an attorney with a strong bias towards the psychologic side of family systems work, I see first-hand how the presence of experts in these other fields working together can make a far greater impact on a family than, let's say a traditional set of attorneys who negotiate a settlement that is positioned and compromised based. Positional bargaining is understood as a traditional form of negotiation where power, influence, or only my needs are the key criteria in getting to a settlement.

In this primer, the reader will gain a deeper look at their own negotiating styles and ways in which they process information. It is important that clients work with counsel who are immersed in interest-based negotiations. Interest based negotiations are understood as a process where the core interests, needs, concerns, hopes, desires, and dreams for the parties involved are heard, understood, and worked through to integrate all sets into one durable and sustainable final agreement.

A major portion of this primer focuses on the role that prior and current life trauma plays in the current conflict. The reader is asked to engage with me in their own experience when connecting the dots between an earlier life trauma, something possibly from childhood or later, and what is occurring in the immediate conflict/dispute you find yourself sitting in.

As a Mediator and Collaborative Lawyer, I am often inspired when I see the power of collaboration at work, realizing that the successful outcomes produced by a thoughtful and focused team of experts are more meaningful than going through a traditional court-ordered process, or some other adversarial process.

This book is primarily written for all of us who have experienced the pain and suffering of being in a difficult family relationship that is no longer tenable. This work translates how the conflict being experienced in the current family relationship might be an opportunity for transformation and healing, both personal and familial.

Caveat – this book is not written from the perspective of a marriage or family counselor aiming at piecing a relationship back together. Rather, the author is an attorney who has been and is dedicated to using the law in a powerful way of structuring settlement agreements for my clients. When my clients realize that from the moment I begin with an intake conversation to a final signed settlement, everything that occurs throughout the process is part of a meaningful transition and transformation.

I am an attorney with a track record of producing durable and creative settlements for my clients. I am also a humanistic/spiritual man who understands the impact that early childhood trauma and adult trauma plays on our neurologic, psychologic, and bio-chemical states of being. When our state of being is rattled over a current event in our lives, we have a rich and beautiful opportunity for growth, no matter how helpless and difficult the situation may seem. My work and understanding of epigenetics, neuroplasticity and spiritual practices all contribute to the content of this book. More than ever, it is imperative that we individually and collectively nurture our awareness of intergenerational trauma, its continued impact on our DNA, and our capacity in healing these deep-seated scars.

Now is the time that clients, attorneys, and all professionals working in the field of family law and family systems adopt a trauma-informed lens for viewing all conflicts. The reason I am so adamant/passionate about this is that in the author's view until our family systems are made whole, our social/organizational systems will not be functioning at their best.

We need our children fully functioning as young adults with the capacity for leadership and serving our nation. Our duty in giving our children the resources and capacity to fulfill their greatest potential lies in their growing up aware of the role that trauma plays in their lives. It is kind of silly to imagine our kids living through two-plus years of a pandemic, losing physical contact with their world, and expecting that there is not going to be some residual trauma carried by them. Add in the increased rate of child, sexual, spousal, and substance abuse, our children may be suffering more than we can imagine. Why is this relevant in relation to this primer and our work in family law: (1) the process that is used to resolve a family system dispute will directly reduce the already difficult separation that is being experienced within the family, and (2) there is a revelatory opportunity for all adults involved in the conflict to emotionally and physically heal whatever the earlier child or adult trauma that might be impinging on the current conflict.

You may be asking, what does any of this have to do with my family conflict? It directly links your decision in selecting the attorney and/or mediator, the type of dispute resolution process you select, and then all steps taken to resolve the matter. In other words, your process, choice, and behavior throughout the process may transform your and your family's life in positive and healthy ways.

DEDICATION

This book is dedicated to my family who every day teach me about love, compassion, and understanding. My wife Jody and our years traversing life's ups and downs together; and my children Arielle and Solly who are my primary teachers in life.

I also dedicate the book to my parents who taught me how to heal in the face of deep grief and how to love in the presence of terror.

DISCLAIMER

This publication is intended to be used for educational purposes only. No legal advice is being given, and no attorney-client relationship is intended to be created by reading this material. The author assumes no liability for any errors or omissions or for how this book or its contents are used or interpreted, or for any consequences resulting directly or indirectly from the use of this book. For legal or any other advice, please consult an experienced attorney or the appropriate expert, who is aware of the specific facts of your case and is knowledgeable in the law in your jurisdiction.

Resolution Matters
Rockville MD: 51 Monroe Street
Suite 1901, 20850
(301) 795-2444
www.resolutionmatters.com

TESTIMONIALS

"I benefited from the services of Steve Shapiro in the mediation of the transfer of assets and ownership for my business when one partner elected to leave the partnership. Steve was broad-minded and nimble in constructing approaches by which we could develop strategies for the transfer. He employed different techniques as appropriate from the several common types of mediation and was a tireless advocate for a process that would leave each partner in the best position possible. Steve has my wholehearted and strongest recommendation!"

– A. Gardner

****

"I just wanted to send you a note to profoundly thank you for holding our hands through this most difficult process and guiding us to the other side- a process and side no one aspires to reach- but sometimes ends up as the only solution. Your humanity, patience, skill, and ability to maintain neutrality were truly outstanding. We would have never gotten here without you. I hope we achieve healing and can rediscover love and appreciation in a rebirth of a new relationship. I trust that this is a possibility if we practice the compassion you always reminded us of. Warmest regards in this difficult time,"

– Diane

****

"Treated me like family. Very respectful and caring. Excellent. No complaints. If you ever have any legal issues, especially with the family he is the right person to speak with and come up with a solution. He listens to your concerns and treats you like a close friend. Thank you, Mr. Shapiro"

– Carmen C.

****

"Steve Shapiro was wonderful he was referred to us and I felt comfortable with my decision with hiring him and he was very respectful of the situation. I had a great experience with Steve Shapiro and will refer friends or family when asked."

– Carie W.

****

"Very good decision. The best, helpful, honest, and very professional person"

– Madhu S.

****

TABLE OF CONTENTS

About The Author

My name is Steve Shapiro and I am a principal with the firm Resolution Matters. I invite you into my practice and my approach to working on family disputes.

I've been in practice for over 30 years, focused on bringing people together, having them work out their differences, and documenting these agreements in the most humane, sensible, and cost-effective way. Separation and divorce, care and decision-making for elder parents, family business matters, and coaching are all within the domain of our practice.

In a divorce setting, bringing the mother and father together to develop a parenting plan, is an essential starting point. Once you have the parenting plan in place it will assist with your schedule, and how much is being paid from one to the other so that you could begin to set up your separate lives together. There's a certain amount of care and concern that gets heard and worked through in those initial stages.

The work in the family business setting is an overlay of emotional issues usually at the intersection of siblings, cousins, nieces, and nephews; typically facing a generational barrier or a lifestyle or values conflict. How you keep a business running and successful in the midst of impending conflict is one fiduciary responsibility owners have, and then planning for a successful future. The mindset and the focus are on being able to bring the family together in whatever way works for their situation.

My practice is based on a fiduciary responsibility to my clients to settle their cases in the most dignified and resourceful way. That's what my commitment is to my clients, in whatever family context it is. We become partners with each other as we do this work. I have the utmost respect for every one of my clients for who they are, and where they are in their lives, and a deep understanding of how difficult it may be at this stage.

CHAPTER 1

GUIDING CLIENTS THROUGH TRAUMATIC FAMILY LAW CASES

"Sweet are the uses of adversity which, like the toad, ugly and venomous, wears yet a precious jewel in his head."
- William Shakespeare

Clients who come to me are not usually living life under what we would consider normal circumstances, but they are certainly not alone in what they are going through. Often my clients who are facing some break up in the family system have suffered through some form of a traumatic event in their life, either sexual abuse, rape, verbal abuse, or some other significant breach in the personal and family system's safety net. Even though this severe episode in someone's life may impact one partner in the relationship more than the other, each partner suffers. This often leaves them unable to continue in an intimate and empowering relationship with their partners. Experience teaches that often we find the abuser came from a family of abuse; a father or mother who was an alcoholic found their parents had their own substance abuse issues. Conversely, a victim can come from a family of abusers, and they are unconsciously perpetuating unhealthy behaviors adopted from their family of origin. This book hopes to capture these scenarios, moving from awareness to a better understanding of how our own scars form the basis for a healthy and flourishing future.

Clients are generally aware and understand how these prior events in their lives impact their current conflict. When they are, it is extremely helpful to the process. Clients become true partners in the process and take responsibility for all aspects of their life's journey. The attorney-client and mediator-client relationships in this situation are foundational. Key values and principles shaping the relationship are trust, open communication, mutual respect, and recognizing a sense of dignity within and around the entire process.

When a client struggles with understanding this nexus and is unable to see this causal relationship that is still an acceptable place to be. When a client is in the place of not knowing the connection between an earlier trauma and their current situation, there is an opportunity to gain the necessary resources and capacity to move with agility through the family breakup/restructure. Of course, not possessing either quality does not disqualify a client from having a smoother transition through the legal process, but it does mean that there may be some resistance and reactivity that might occur. This situation is perfectly fine too.

My work with clients is informed by the Japanese art of Kintsugi or repairing broken vessels. The Japanese artist is capable of sealing together broken chards from a vase with gold inlay, causing a more beautiful entity to form than before. In my experience, the marriage of the law and trauma are intertwined. Our Bar Associations owe a responsibility to find ways to truly resolve conflict while implementing law and order. My family law practice forms such a union where each individual client feels that they are more whole and ready for a new start. In an ideal world, your family members would offer you the best wishes and blessings for this new start in life. Most important for me is that each client knows that they have moved through an important stage in their lives and they appreciate where they have come from, trust that the best process was used to settle their issues, and we worked to come up with the best possible solutions for the situation.

The Key Take-Aways:

We are living through traumatic times and all its permutations:

Okay let's take a pause and I ask that you join me on the balcony. We are going to take several trips back and forth up to the balcony. It is as good a time as any to build this understanding and awareness into your gut, that when you move above the stage of your life, you can gain space, clarity, and wisdom - - simply during a few breaths.

Why am I reading about trauma when I am in the middle of a family crisis and need a lawyer? Any family system crisis, by virtue of its definition, is cloaked in trauma. When we work together, you are extended a warm welcome to join me on the balcony and gain a broader perspective of your dispute.

The work we do in the attorney-client, or mediator-client relationship provides an opportunity for clients to start anew. The distinction is that we cannot be driving down the road with our hands on the rearview mirror. If clients are gripping the past either for revenge or some other place of pain, they may need therapeutic assistance. It may pay to negotiate a pause in the legal proceedings for the client to get some professional assistance in this situation. Or at a minimum, work concurrently in the process.

This leads to recognition of the role of therapists, CPAs, and other professionals in the process. We will refer throughout this book to the collaborative law model or hybrid mediation models, all utilizing a multi-skilled professional model to bring the best of the best to resolve your family system issue. As an attorney/mediator/and student of how trauma impacts conflict and family systems, I am a champion of this approach. As the United Nations recently found that the Collaborative Law divorce model is the most humane and sustainable form of a divorce settlement in the world, so might it fit your situation.

Readers will gain wisdom by understanding that by identifying earlier life's traumas, you might find that it was not even your trauma, but a family or ancestral trauma causing the current upset. In any case, being human means, we have appropriately numbed ourselves from not fully moving into the pain, especially when we were young. When we gain more awareness, begin to accept, and transmute these experiences into our bodies so that they dissipate, we gain power, resource, and agency. The client gains more capacity and agency for dealing effectively with this difficult situation.

Traditional matrimonial law tends to lean into an adversarial process because the natural order of things is that when we don't deal with these traumas, we move into a reactive state and become more aggressive and angrier, and the clients transfer this anger to anyone close to them. The lawyer then must step up to control the emotional intensity with his or her counterpart. In turn, this step up the emotional intensity with the other spouse, and then you are in this vicious cycle of reactivity. In the traditional settlement process, it translates into tens of thousands of dollars being spent on depositions, document requests, interrogatories, and all the investigative costs that go on in a difficult family breakup.

When we enter a conversation about earlier challenging events, even for a moment, there is a likelihood of reducing reactivity and increasing the opportunity for transformation. Why is transformation important? It is the key ingredient in restructuring. In the above paragraph discussing the consequences of litigation, we show how a process-driven out of reactivity and anger will not only break the bank, it will also break the emotional bank where any opportunity for real communication will take years to heal, if at all.

You will have all the legal settlement documents you need at the end of the process to move on. How you move on, not dragging this past chapter, but instead stepping into anew, is the question.

CHAPTER 2

TUNING INTO THE MENTAL AND EMOTIONAL STATE OF THE CLIENT

"When it is dark enough, you can see the stars."

– Ralph Waldo Emerson

Our clients are healthy, constructive individuals and generally, they are trying to work through the parameters of a family dispute in a way that they can start anew. They would like their children taken care of and protected. In the beginning, they come to me without malicious thoughts for their family members/spouse in the beginning. Often though, when we hit some triggers, they begin to show vulnerability, fear, and anxiety about what might come.

The more Clients can experience being understood and recognized for who they are, they will know they are not alone. They should be reminded that hundreds of thousands of people in that situation have already gone through what they are experiencing and come out okay. We are going to work together.

Clients Do Not Typically Apprise the Details That Led Them to This Point in Life . . . But that is the essence of the journey.

An exercise that I encourage clients to practice is what I teach at a course on dealing with difficult people and is taught in many leadership courses as well. I suggest an exercise based on Going to the Balcony. It is the concept of going on a balcony where you can observe everything occurring on the stage of your life and in your relationships. Then you bring that difficult relationship up to the balcony. You sit with that individual with who you are in conflict within this imaginary space. You then visualize listening to this person who is challenging you.

It could be a boss, it could be your child, it could be anybody, but in this situation, it's your family member/spouse. You really listen and ask them what's going on. Conversely, you can share what is going on with you right now? What's important to you? You try to listen consciously, but you also try to listen in a thought field where you've been living with this person as children or as a spouse or partner, for 5 years, 10 years, 20 years, however long you have known one another. You want to hear from them and you want to be able to restate it back so that they hear it from you. Then you want to imagine that your partner is asking you the same important question, what are your interests right now? What's concerning you as we go through this process? This is an ongoing question and exchange throughout the entire process. The idea is that by rehearsing in the balcony, you will be a lot less charged and reactive when you begin discussions/negotiations with this individual.

The point of this exercise is not that you are scheming about how to get at this individual. You are invoking a sense of honor, relationship, and appreciation for the individual for being in your life. What I find is that too many people at the time of a family breakup begin to really get tough on themselves. We are our worst enemies because we are so hard on ourselves and we make ourselves wrong for having chosen this family or this individual. How come I didn't know? I should have known; I should have seen the signals. Well okay, but the truth is you spent however many years with this individual. Can we heal that relationship so you move on and you don't drag that baggage into that next relationship? That's also true for not dragging that baggage into a co-parenting relationship that may last for another 15 years depending on the age of the children.

This is a recurring exercise that I encourage my clients to practice throughout the dispute-resolution process.

Finding the Balance Between Engaging and Connecting with Clients

In order to keep a professional distance, I practice staying objective and detached. As an attorney and mediator, I do not own the client's issues. I do not say that in a negative way or non-caring way, but for personal health and effectiveness. I can do this and also still really lean into my clients to empathize and understand what is happening in their situations. In order to remain open and transparent, I practice co-regulation. This is the ability to be with the client in a way that they feel deeply understood and listened to.

The best metaphor I have heard for co-regulating is to imagine we are two trains traveling on two parallel train tracks. The purpose of co-regulating our breathing, for example, is that we create a greater level of coherence and understanding between each of our nervous systems. If I am traveling 40 mph and you are traveling 65 mph, we are out of sync. If I can increase my system's breath to something approaching 65 mph, you may begin feeling heard and respected quite differently than before. When we settle into this co-regulated model we find that each individual is unique, special, gifted, and talented. They also have an incredible capacity to do wonderful things. Yes, even in the face of conflict.

CHAPTER 3

DEFINING TRAUMA IN THE CONTEXT OF FAMILY LAW

"Every Challenge That We Run into Is Actually a Call of Life For Us to Connect Deeper. Every Challenge is Part of Our Teacher."
- Thomas Hubl

Understanding how trauma and conflict intertwine, potentially exacerbating differences within a family system, are key to the client and their family's success. When we address a client's concerns in the context of past and present trauma, they become better prepared before entering triggering and upsetting situations like a collaborative law or mediation setting, let alone a courtroom. My team uses the factors that comprise trauma to best understand our client's needs. This information becomes indispensable when we are engaged in working on a case together.

How do we define trauma in the context of family law cases? When an individual has endured a traumatic event, such as the loss of a loved one, the loss of a job, sexual abuse, incest, substance, alcohol, verbal, or many other types of abuse, these experiences get internalized. Other factors can include multigenerational and collective trauma. Multigenerational trauma is the cause of many unwanted life situations. History repeats itself unless we are able to address and transmute the underlying causes of trauma. My clients all have an instinctual resilience and coping capacity. People are generally effective at being able to continue to function in the real world even after having experienced serious life-threatening conditions.

A recent client who we will call Sharon shared with me that her mom and dad had divorced when she was ten years old. Her mother had an affair and her dad left the mother, paid her nothing in the settlement/divorce, and their lives carried on. The challenge here is that the young girl, now an adult woman in her fifties with two grown children, learns that her husband was having an affair. Does she play out the same pattern that her father did, and expel her husband from her life as her father responded to her mother? Thankfully, Sharon had enough self-awareness to realize that her husband was a vital player in her adult children's life and that completely alienating him would not help anyone. The story illustrates that our patterns and behaviors formed at earlier stages in life help shape our current attitudes and beliefs.

When a client has experienced a recent traumatic experience, we view that it has a potential stacking quality with events occurring in the present day. The cumulative impact of past trauma is viewed as an iceberg – every experience that could be viewed as traumatic, stacks itself, like another layer of ice on top of the older layers. If we can identify those earlier experiences that contain a roadmap of how we were victimized and how we have learned to separate ourselves from our feelings, we might be able to begin creating a new narrative and some real healing.

Let me introduce you to Sam who graduated from the Naval Academy and became a fighter pilot in Afghanistan. Sam became a wounded warrior both from the abuse she had experienced at the Naval Academy as well as the brutality of war. By the time Sam came home, there were not a lot of available options for processing PTSD and the associated reactive behavior that goes along with the psychic and emotional pain experiences. Instead, she did what most Americans are good at, wound up throwing herself into her work and an exciting romance. Sam met Tony soon after he arrived home and their emotional and psychic vulnerabilities attracted one another.

Tony wound up having his own traumas having been raised by two felons, brought up in foster homes, and through that challenge, became a self-made man. He started multiple successful business platforms, partnered with Sam in building the vision for the business, and brought three beautiful children into the world.

As we are learning, the more circumstances that cause an older traumatic event to get triggered, the more the unconscious mind triggers not our best selves. Suffice it to say that Sam and Tony began clashing over most decisions in their life. This led Tony who exhibits some severe narcissistic tendencies to act out often belligerently at Sam, causing her to retreat only to avoid his seeming abuse. This was turning into an unhealthy relationship.

As Sam began taking on a deep understanding of her earlier narratives, she was open to the possibility for these prior harmful experiences to no longer play a detrimental role in her health and well-being. This resulted in a sense of purpose, renewal, and hope to manifest from the depths of traumatic experiences that were previously frozen.

In our discussions, we can bring awareness to these earlier traumas. By recognizing it, we simply bring some thoughtfulness when working with a client of trauma. We can label it, identify it, and not judge it. We can also support the family member in not blaming themselves for what's occurred.

In Sharon's case, it would be easy to fall into the victim role as her father did. Studies show that childhood trauma can transfer through the DNA to a second or third generation. Not only do I believe that

Sharon had a sense of responsibility for her own welfare, but also that of her adult children in not repeating the mistakes of her parents. Family systems may be one area in our lives where this pattern plays out the strongest.

Trauma victims become a bit paralyzed, even freeze or lose their power when they are in a conference with the abuser. I find this often with my clients, largely with women, where they come to me searching for their voice and somehow their voice has been stuffed away because of the stacking of negative experiences of abuse. We want to bring more awareness to those experiences in recognizing that that individual, the client, is not responsible at all for the abuse. It is a circumstance they're living in or have just separated from, or maybe it was as a family of origin, and it's impacting their intimate relations today. We want to just name it and bring awareness and attention to it. In doing so, the client can metabolize those earlier experiences and then move on.

CHAPTER 4

HOW TRAUMA INDICATORS INFLUENCE FAMILY TRANSFORMATION

"Family Should Be the Place Where You Can Be Your Most Complete Self."
-Oprah Winfrey

Sometimes, the indicators of trauma are not clear or easy to pick out. My family law clients come into the conversation generally fully functioning adults in society, succeeding in their profession/business and in their parenting role. Then through questions and building relationships, the client feels a sense of safety and begins to open up a little.

Clients could also express anger, depression, anxiety, and all the emotional stressors that are causing them to not be as fully functioning as they could be. They're beginning to realize that there is something triggering them. Together in a safe space, we try to put our arms around and figure out what that might be. Again, not as a therapeutic model, but as a constructive conversation supporting them in this important life transition. We are working together to resolve a long-standing family dispute, not resolve some earlier childhood or inter-generational trauma. Yet understanding how the two are and could be inextricably related does assist dramatically in resolving the matter. Most clients come to me, not with an idea for a band-aid, but seeking legal action causing a major life change.

A client, let's call her Nancy, comes to me after having been raped and is having difficulty finding intimacy with her partner. The partner is asking for a divorce because of this. Through a series of questions, the trauma comes up. "What caused the breakup?" "What are they experiencing?" "What shame might they be experiencing in this breakup?" We know historically around divorce, there's always some degree of shame for just going through the separation/divorce process. I ask about the cause of that shame and find it's often not so much about the public image as it is a feeling of failure. A victim in an abusive situation or relationship often carries a sense of failure that, "I caused this". In Nancy's case, she was working in therapy, she understood the intergenerational traumatic aspect of her experience and entered a collaborative divorce process to best protect and strengthen her goals in starting new in the world.

This shame can create an enabling behavior, that leads to one form or another of domestic violence. Note, that domestic violence victims are not the only ones who suffer from trauma. The abuser is also likely suffering from some earlier trauma. It is unfortunate that our culture and society does not often uncover the causes of trauma in the abuser until it is too late. The abuser's trauma is more acute in a domestic violence case, increasing the safety and health risks for the abused spouse and family members.

In any situation, it is safe to conclude that all family law clients carry some earlier trauma with them into the legal process. The most courageous act they can do is be vulnerable and share with their counsel about these earlier events. Counsel's job is not to judge, but to ensure that their client is receiving the necessary support they need at the moment to make it through this legal proceeding.

Long-Term Physiological Effects of Trauma

The lasting effect of trauma is like you are continuously dragging a weight with no break. In trauma discussions, it's sometimes viewed as an iceberg. That the stacks of experiences of abuse or traumatic events stack on top of one another, but we only see the bit that's on the surface.

The foundational piece of trauma is often in our family of origin. I view that an individual's superpowers exist within some of those earlier times when they experienced abuse or something traumatic, like a death or a loss of a parent. I've seen this with myself, as I have worked with those who lost their fathers when they were young. They tend to have not processed the loss fully. Then they come into a family conflict with a lot of pent-up anger because of their loss and grief they never fully resolved. These feelings show up in how they parent, possibly because they didn't have that role model to guide them. Unconsciously, this anger or grief directs how they parent and how they can feel comfortable in their manhood. This may show up as unhealthy behaviors all too often impacting the other spouse and children.

A practice tip for all professionals, attorneys, et. al., is the importance of processing these earlier traumas in our own preparatory work. As counsel, we are more effective when our partnership and alliance with our clients are fully functioning and healthy. For the relationship to be successful, it functions best when all individuals involved, including counsel, are aware of, and resolved to not let their past traumas impact the current work.

As an eight-year-old experiencing my father's near death with a major heart attack, I understand what it is like for an adult father today who is separating or going through a family business breakup, or any number of conflicts in life. In this situation, I understand what might stem from a combination of how that eight-year-old boy dealt with the separation, grief, fear, and vulnerability - - and protected himself with busyness, avoidance, and denial. There is a deeper understanding that a father who lost his father at a young age might have a hard time separating. It is difficult enough for professionals to have a larger understanding of the client's life, let alone not feel victimized or retraumatized through this legal process.

Physical symptoms could show up in children being unable to process early trauma. Children may develop any number of ailments as a way of coping and not address the underlying cause such as one parent or both parents acting in ways that are not kind and compassionate towards one another.

The long-term impacts of trauma are carried over from their childhood and they may find themselves struggling in their parenting role. I spend time with young families in setting up a parenting plan, working on each of their mutual responsibilities, and the effects of their behavior on their children. But this is when they're coming to me to help separate and develop this child access plan or parenting plan; this is after the fact. We're all dealing with the effect of what may have occurred that caused their anger, frustration, and lack of patience with the other.

The long-term effects of traumatic events are vast. It's been demonstrated scientifically that these effects are being carried over to the second or third generation from the first generation's traumatic experiences. We can see how it plays out with Sharon and her decision not to try alienating her husband from his kids the way her father did with her mother. One of the hopes that I have in my work is to bring attention to this pattern of trauma where it is nobody's fault. If we don't bring awareness to it, we are continuing to perpetuate some of these dysfunctions. There is an opportunity for the client, the family, the attorney, and the whole team of people who are working to support the resolution.

What Are the Physical Effects of Trauma?

There are more obvious long-term physical effects of trauma. Let's look at a veteran of war who comes home after losing a limb. They may have been fitted with the most advanced artificially intelligent limb you can imagine, but they're still going to have a memory of that traumatic event. Their body is going to have a memory of that missing limb. Although the trauma is in the past, the body does not forget.

Studies show traumatic experiences may affect our physical body. Interestingly, when someone says they have stage fright and they can't breathe, one of the reasons is that we carry most of our nerves and nerve endings in the belly region. A person who is in the middle of re-experiencing a trauma, like a family law client who is in the middle of a difficult negotiation, may shut down breathing, by not getting oxygen pumped through the blood to the brain. This reaction to trauma causes us to become more anxious and physically less healthy.

Trauma experts have spent time focusing on breathing to assist patients with gaining more resilience.

As an attorney, we can do this with clients, even without having to delve into what the situation may be. The physical health and benefit of belly breathing is an excellent remedy for what otherwise could be increased mental, emotional, or physical stress on the body.

When we're triggered, all-of-a-sudden we're losing our sense of communication and our sense of intimacy. When this happens, we lose our ability to relate to another person with a deep sense of respect and honor. When this occurs, meaning someone's earliest traumas go unchecked, it may breed narcissism and other self-indulgent behaviors. What we're trying to prevent is the repeating of these old patterns.

CHAPTER 5

MORAL AND LEGAL PRINCIPLES OF TRAUMA IN FAMILY LAW

"The pain body wants to survive, just like every other entity in existence, and it can only survive if it gets you to unconsciously identify with it."
- Eckhart Tolle

There is a moral and ethical approach to dealing with some very difficult conversations in family law. One example is a client who is having an affair and they're committed to continuing the affair, although they recognize the harm that is being done to their spouse. At this point, we could go full-stop and recognize there's a whole study of moral and legal principles at play in this example. When there's evidence of adultery, depending on the jurisdiction, it's going to be a factor in the divorce. In Maryland, for example, it's one of 12 factors that's going to be looked at in shaping alimony. It's not going to be an all-consuming factor but it's going to be looked at. In an adversarial breakup, we may often see private investigators that are aimed at shaming the cheating spouse and ultimately using it as leverage in their divorce settlement. Simply the conversation about an individual committing adultery in terms of the integrity of the marital vows recognizes there is a breach. If there's continuing bad behavior that's being done secretly, punitively, or maliciously, then that could raise the stakes of an award of alimony depending on the circumstances of the couple and the family.

This could also apply to embezzlement of funds from marital assets. The spouse who depletes marital funds either out of spite, greed, or anger, has some serious moral, ethical, and legal challenges to face. The whole concept of using a mediative or collaborative approach is to transmute and transform the emotional states to avoid one spouse from taking things too far and sabotaging any remaining goodwill that exists in the relationship. In this set of circumstances, trust is not easily restored, and reaching a holistic settlement is going to be challenging.

In the case of Roberto and Carmen, the former was identified as having an affair, and knowledge about this was communicated in front of their 7 and 10 year old daughters. Is there any way Carmen could ever trust Roberto again? In this case, through multiple challenging mediation sessions, an apology came forth from Roberto to Carmen and the affair ended. Was this a continuing traumatic event for Carmen? Was it an original traumatic event for the children who were witnesses to their mother learning of this for the first time?

There are several moral factors addressed in family law. Often clients may say, "We're divorcing and we're separating. I want to be able to see and date, but I don't want to do that unless I know I have permission given that we're separated". This is an adult form of behavior. To raise that issue, to address the issue, and see what concerns there are. When there are children involved, this will factor into the parenting plan. It factors into the types of conversations about when to introduce someone to the children or should you introduce them to your soon-to-be-ex-spouse first? How long should you be dating before introducing the children? A whole series of questions comes out about the welfare of the children and how they should be exposed to the new partner.

Another example of a moral topic in family law is the role of the gatekeeper. The gatekeeper is one parent that has the children and looks for excuses or reasons to keep the children away from the other spouse and/or grandparents to be malicious. The moral and ethical piece here is clear. The best interest of the children is to be exposed to each parent for as much time as they can, as well as the grandparents. This is presuming that each of these individuals is a healthy, functioning adult, and is not putting the children in harm's way. But the question is, are they gatekeeping to be abusive because of some sort of trauma that they experienced as a child that's showing up in this form or something else? Again, this is an important inquiry for professionals to have and not avoid.

We could take a step back from both the affair and the depletion of marital assets and ask, "What were the behaviors that might have caused someone to do that? What were they so afraid of that they couldn't, in a healthy way, raise their concerns with their spouse? What happened to prevent them from being respectful and honoring this person that they vowed to stay true to?" These are questions a mediator and/or a collaborator should be having with the spouse if these activities were occurring during the separation process.

The use of an interim agreement is an available procedural method to incorporate understandings reached between spouses or partners as they proceed through the rest of the separation or divorce process. In other words, all outstanding and preliminary issues can get addressed in order to maintain balance and cooperative behavior. We could cover that without having to go to court. We could work through those issues and come up with an interim agreement that's going to be a thoughtful, meaningful approach to how the couple is going to work together as they go through this divorce process. You can imagine that if you don't have that type of agreement to start the process, then everything else on top of that is going to be about who is to blame for the situation and we'd continue to act on top of those broken agreements that we started with.

CHAPTER 6

UNIDENTIFIED TRAUMA AND A FAMILY LAW CASE

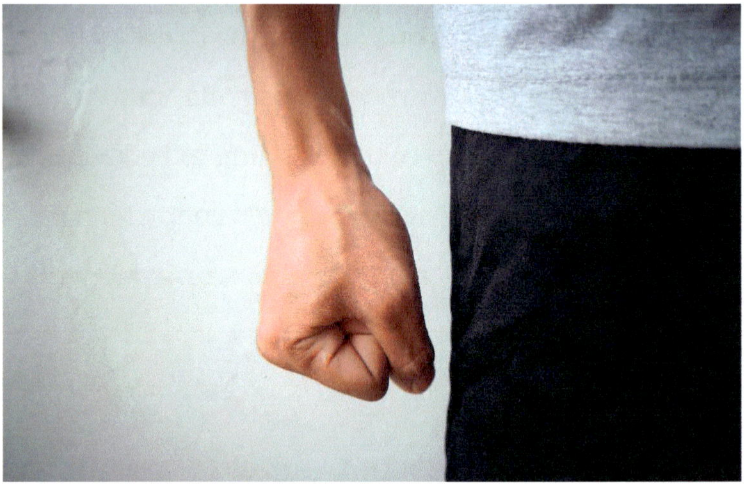

"When We Are Not Fully Present, We Are Not Really Living."

- Thich Nhat Hanh

When working with a client, it's very challenging when trauma can't be identified. One of my roles is to bring a sense of awareness to every client. I'm aware that anyone walking in the door, who I'm serving as their attorney or mediator, has experienced some form of trauma. With or without their cooperation or awareness, I'm going to work with them.

However, if the effect of trauma is so deep and horrific and impacts a client's ability to function in a mutual relational way, even with their attorney, I'm not going to put myself through that... nor should any attorney put themselves in an abusive relationship. If it's not detected, the attorney or mediator may be the recipient of that transference of anger and hostility because it's how that client is wired.

Not every case is the right one and, in those cases, I could easily refer clients to someone else. It happens too often, but preferably I would want to identify and work with the client to figure out what might be causing their outburst.

Working With People Who Have Experienced Trauma

The Rules of Professional Conduct that states an attorney must represent their client zealously has to include building trauma awareness into their practice. While situations that bring a client into my office might be causing much upset, added trauma outside of that can cause concern for their mental health. The healthier the client is, the more capacity the client has. If they are less reactive, the more they oversee their own fate and are able to resolve the matter with an experienced attorney by their side. The counsel and coaches working with the client are able to observe transformational moments when the clients begin to understand and put this work into practice.

Because lawyers are trained to go after facts and data, they may lose sight of the well-being of the client at times. Once the discovery or litigation process begins, the client can become overwhelmed with demands from their attorney, the other family member, and work/community demands of others. This dynamic needs to be examined in the preliminary stages when determining the best method for resolving the family dispute. If in a divorce matter, the other spouse holds all the accounts and records and is not sharing this information, a mediated or collaborative law process is not the proper method for solving this case. It is usually in these situations that I might refer the case to a colleague who will work with the client in a litigation format to demand discovery of all the family's financial records to ascertain and come to a fair/equitable settlement.

Before I even consider getting all the facts and data for a client's case, I need to find out who this person is, what makes them tick, what caused the family to break up, etc. Then we can best determine and recommend the type of settlement methodology that is best for their situation.

Separate Emotions From The Law When Analyzing Legal Problems

Attorneys are trained to be advocates for their clients, to represent their clients fully and uncover all the facts that are necessary to put together the best case in their client's interests. This means that an attorney is trained to get the facts at any cost. It may cause protracted, extended discovery, and may cause higher costs of litigation. What we find is that most attorneys are, because of this training, going to do what they need to do to gain complete discovery, despite fully understanding the nuances and the impacts on their clients' overall mental and emotional health, and considering what the long-term impacts may be on the client's relationship to the rest of the family. Certainly, the trend over the last 20-30 years in using more mediation and collaborative law practices has created a new opportunity for lawyers to gain more awareness and thoughtfulness around these issues and tensions that we are addressing.

Lawyers who passionately represent their clients, instruct their clients on all avenues and processes that are available to them. In other words, attorneys have a duty to explain to their clients all the different processes, including mediation, collaborative law, arbitration, and traditional settlement litigation, and really spend time upfront with them examining all the pros and cons of each of those choices. This is a key point. The more attorneys speak with their clients and have a healthy back and forth and listen carefully to what the client's interests are, they can design together what should be a successful process for them to resolve this family dispute.

If a client comes in with their mind made up about what they want to do, then the attorney can certainly listen to that and try to ask questions and express his or her opinion about that. Depending on the facts, circumstances, and the state of the client, I may or may not choose to work with the client. There have been many cases where I do not feel like the chemistry or the philosophical perspective is shared mutually between the client and myself at that point, and that is okay. It is better for the client and for the attorney to know upfront that this is not a good working relationship than to spend thousands and thousands of dollars only to realize later that this wasn't a good fit.

CHAPTER 7

EFFECTS TRAUMATIZED CLIENTS HAVE ON ATTORNEYS

"The Peace We Can Aspire To Then Is Not A Harmonious Peace Of The Grave, Nor A Submissive Peace Of The Slave, But A Hard Working Peace Of The Brave."
- William Ury

The Third Side: Why We Fight And How We Can Stop

All family law attorneys have spent their careers dealing with difficult issues such as standing in the middle of marital and family conflicts. It is a difficult area of law to navigate, and family lawyers have a bad reputation in society. Often attorneys can get triggered by their clients' circumstances. Because of this, it is advisable that family law attorneys go through training for dealing with clients experiencing trauma. This will allow the attorneys to be present when working with clients whose situations might otherwise trigger them emotionally.

At Resolution Matters, we use the practice of mindfulness, where we can sit with the client and be present while attending to the client's circumstances without being retraumatized ourselves. If we are reminded of our own trauma or a person who caused the trauma, we might transfer our own feelings onto the client or another party involved in the case. Mindfulness can help protect us and the clients from that happening.

Vicarious Trauma and The Family Law Attorney

Vicarious trauma comes from being traumatized by hearing the stories of others. For example, a lawyer who is working with people who were present at 9/11 might hear so many brutal stories of that day that they feel as if they experienced the same thing as the client, therefore also becoming traumatized.

Because of possible vicarious trauma, family lawyers need to set healthy boundaries, while also remaining empathetic. It can be difficult to keep that balance. A family lawyer must remain distanced enough so that they don't traumatize themselves while listening empathetically.

A family law practice is not for everyone. Practicing attorneys play a crucial role in assisting clients in getting back on their feet and moving into life again feeling more grounded and focused than before. As discussed earlier, when an attorney is triggered because of a client's actions that may be driven by some recent or past traumatic event in their life, mindfulness can help the attorney maintain that balance. Mindfulness is not used here as some catch-all phrase imagining it will solve all problems. More specifically, when an attorney and/or client go to the balcony to observe the situation, they can draw strength and guidance by detaching from the situation and gaining a greater awareness from afar. This is a mindfulness practice, taught to executives who are dealing with conflict situations. In the family law arena, we assist our clients by suggesting that by observing the conflict and your reactions to it, there lies the possibility that you can reduce the charge it has over you.

In the case of the two brothers who were in a paper mill business in Louisiana, one brother was continually, yet unintendedly making fun of his younger brother. When working with the brothers it seemed like everyone's desire was to work things out between the brothers so they can join back together in running the mill. However, the more we were able to calm the level of reactivity amongst the brothers, they both were able to realize that maybe it was better to split up the ownership. It was not the outcome they thought they wanted at the beginning of the process, but it was the outcome that seemed appropriate given their individual development cycle. The individual development is an important lens in family disputes because often adults have not separated from the family dynamic of their parents and may perpetuate older unhealthy patterns. This is so as long as the social patterns remain in place.

Work To Ensure That Your Emotional and Physical Limits Aren't Exceeded In These Cases

I must remind myself that the service I provide to my clients has a sense of purpose and mission that is greater than myself. It is paramount that I take care of my clients' welfare. In doing so, I must also practice self-care.

Epigenetics is the notion that one recognizes that they have past trauma. For instance, one might have suffered a loss in the family as a child. If it isn't recognized and healed, that sense of loss and suffering then could become generational. By healing the hurt, we can shift the genetic make-up so that the trauma is not passed down through generations.

Epigenetics is linked to an area of neuropsychology called neuroplasticity of the brain. Neuroplasticity suggests that through language, nutrition, sleep, water, and healthy behaviors, we can begin to establish new patterns in the brain to create new ways of being. Being aware of epigenetics and neuroplasticity will help a lawyer become a better coach for their clients.

I know you may be asking what any of this has to do with family law. It is actually at the heart of it. An effective family law outcome, whether through settlement or court order, is aimed at having a clean slate for the parties to start a new life. Family lawyers will be the first to tell you that if you keep doing the same things repeatedly, you will likely get the same results. This means all clients have an opportunity for transformation and real personal growth/development if they see it and take it. Without having some guidance and awareness about how past abuse or harm could repeat itself and cause future harm, a client and counsel might be not only dealing with a difficult opposing client but a difficult client as well. Our job is to reduce the fears, tension, and stress surrounding our client representation.

Attorneys Must Take Care of Him or Herself When Working On These Difficult Cases

We see how rapidly things change in our society, how technology changes, how medicine changes, how law changes, and how relationships change. The more equipped an attorney is to take care of himself, the better he can support his clients. Attorneys are encouraged to learn some self-reflection techniques so they can check in with their own reactions to a client's story. The balcony metaphor works especially well for attorneys who are struggling with a difficult client. Observe what is reacting inside you to their behavior, language, and story. Be gentle with yourself and give yourself permission to observe without judgment what arises for you. Whatever it might be, don't ignore it. Pay careful attention as this may become a great teacher and guide for you as you move forward with this and future clients. However, most important is your care and capacity to reduce your own reactivity and be even more effective in dealing with challenging client matters.

CHAPTER 8

DEALING WITH VICTIMS OF TRAUMA AND DELICATE TOPICS

"Because No Matter How Hard A Conversation Is, I Know That On The Other Side Of That Difficult Conversation Lies Peace. Knowledge. An Answer Is Delivered. Character Is Revealed. Truces Are Formed. Misunderstandings Resolved."
– Shonda Rhimes

Every client who comes in to consider working with me has a story and a specific set of needs and interests. The initial meeting is key to finding out what their triggers might be. Each client shares about their existing relations and how they communicate with one another. This gives insight into whether the client can even speak to the other parties involved, whether on the phone or in person. This will indicate whether mediation might be possible. After that, the differences among mediation, collaborative law, traditional settlement, and litigation are discussed. A party's mental health can impact the entire process. Attorneys who can demonstrate empathy and compassion are necessary for this process. Mental health treatment might be suggested to resolve some cases.

If a client is severely debilitated and not functioning well due to their relationship, that is the time to ask whether they are receiving mental health treatment. If they are not, it might be suggested that they do so. They are asked to work with a lawyer and a mental health professional to resolve the issues.

It can be difficult to bring awareness to these mental health matters. Often, people are ashamed to talk about it, and that is why the traumatized person becomes the victim too often. The goal is to move the client from the feeling of being a victim to finding their voice. They need to be able to speak without aggression and speak with honesty and truth so that their interests are met. This is key to building capacity, strength, and the client's ability to remain an active participant in this often rigorous process.

As discussed above, when I teach a class on dealing with difficult people I often use the metaphor of going to the balcony. It is a mindfulness exercise, where I instruct the client in some restful moment; maybe before going to bed or just waking up in the morning, but the client needs to have a clear mind. The client should establish a place where they are the observer of what is going on in their life and this difficult situation. This balcony becomes very present throughout the entire process because every time that the client anticipates moving into any form of interaction or challenge, the balcony is always available for them to separate themselves from how they may be charged emotionally by the other party.

On the balcony, I instruct my clients to imagine the person who they are having difficulty with sitting next to and begin listening to the other person speak. This all happens in their imagination, but it re-establishes that rapport and an understanding where they can begin to really listen to what is going on with the other person, and the other person is feeling heard and listened to. The same thing happens in reverse. It's reciprocal and mutual, where the other relation begins to listen to the client and understands and hears them deeply. This occurs even in the most difficult and longest estranged relationships you can imagine. It really works and there is a shift in the relationship. I could extend that out even further and really begin where the client sees themselves on the balcony with the other person. They begin to move towards each other and they continue this mutual conversation. Maybe there is even an exchange of forgiveness, but it is repeated a number of times. It is like meditation so that there really is the possibility of healing taking place. If you can bring some awareness to that earlier trauma, you have a much greater probability and the possibility of resolving the conflict at hand. The most significant benefit being in the balcony is to separate ourselves from the problem, gain perspective and objectivity so we can be less reactive moving into negotiations and life.

There is a concept in the field of trauma called co-regulation, discussed earlier in this primer, and is probably not well known in the legal world. When on the balcony, one begins to regulate one's breathing and nervous system around the other person's breathing and nervous system. This practice settles both parties' grounding and enables them to be with one another. In addition, there will be a deeper reception of what is said and shared. The client then sets boundaries and communication that work. When a client feels more comfortable in their own skin, they are more comfortable with the legal process.

Avoid Re-Traumatizing A Client While Getting Information

Building the client's capacity to be present, fluid, open-minded, and resourceful is the goal while recognizing the relationship between trauma and the current conflict. There is always a risk of some re-traumatization during family disputes. Hopefully, the process will help the client begin to develop self-care skills so that they see the trauma and not stay in it for as long. The key is to develop skills so that the client does not remain entrenched in the state of being a victim.

With new skills, we are able to change states more quickly and become more present in the moment and where we need to be. If we remain in a negative state, we are not available to others. If the client builds capacity, the more the client can be responsive to the demands of the case.

Therapy and Mental Health Counseling for Clients with Traumatic Experiences

In many cases, clients are referred to me by a therapist, another lawyer, rabbi, or minister. When they are referred by a therapist, it is apparent that the client is working on themselves and has some awareness of their own and their family members' issues. If they are not receiving mental health treatment and they have been in a traumatic event, I will have a conversation with them broaching the subject of therapy.

Even though there is therapist-client confidentiality, a client's mental capacity will come into play if there is litigation. The court might order a child assessment and a parent interview. During mediation and collaborative processes, a mental health professional assists as a coach supporting the client through the family law proceeding. The mediation and/or collaborative law approach to family dispute settlement may not be perfect, and it holds a possibility for clients to be heard, understood, and potentially resolve core issues standing in the way of moving on in their lives.

CHAPTER 9

KEY TRAITS OF TRAUMA INFORMED LAWYERING

"Injustice Anywhere Is a Threat to Justice Everywhere"

– Martin Luther King, Jr.

It is tantamount to compare it to the cancer industry where chemotherapy may get rid of cancer, but it also might kill the patient. We see over the last 20 - 30 years, how the scientific community is fine-tuning that balance to try to save life and not just kill everything in its sight through chemo. Similarly, the legal profession is learning that the extensiveness of litigation has its own effects. We know that courts get backlogged, judges and lawyers get burnt out, and we know that having overloaded dockets cause an institutional lens to hear a client's case if they are in that system.

All that said, the way the traditional legal system is set up, there is no room and space for considering the role that trauma plays on individuals in the system. Overlay the criminal law framework and possibilities of racial violence among other issues, and how traumatized does the individual become? It crosses into civil law and family law matters. This is one strong reason for the burgeoning of mediation and collaborative law throughout the US and Canada in particular.

Trauma-informed lawyering addresses the needs of the client over the needs of the system. This happens when a trauma-informed lawyer can sit, pay attention, and establish rapport and a deep understanding of the client's interests, needs, and concerns. Clients are much healthier and happier. When a trauma-informed lawyer takes this approach, he or she will try to navigate to get the best possible settlement for their clients without causing an all-out war. In a trauma-informed environment, we are looking at the intersection between where the current conflict sits in relation to where the trauma began. When clients and their attorneys can do this together, it is profound.

The topic of attorney burnout and vicarious trauma concerns are currently being addressed at the American Bar Association and State Bar Associations. Lawyers are realizing that if they relate more with their clients, they can often come up with settlement outcomes that best support their clients. Much attorney burnout is due to poor client relationships, particularly client dissatisfaction, which is not good for client/lawyer relationships, the law firm's growth, and the public's view of the legal system. Attorney resilience is important as well. The Bar Associations are spending more time and effort to provide training for attorneys to gain resilience, deeper awareness, and appreciation for their clients, especially with the increased societal complexities we are facing.

There are various forms of trauma that attorneys should be aware of; intergenerational trauma, collective trauma, historical trauma, and family trauma. We have already addressed the notion of how intergenerational trauma can play out in a family dispute. William Ury, the co-founder of the Harvard Negotiation Project at Harvard Law School, supports the notion in "Getting to Yes With Yourself," that the attorney or other professionals must make sure their needs and interests are being met in the attorney-client relationship.

The more capacity in which an attorney can claim ownership for major trauma in their own life, the more capacity and compassion they will have for a deep understanding of their client's concerns. This is not easy work, but the attorney and/or professionals who take this on will be the better for it.

CHAPTER 10

EFFECTIVE WAYS TO DEAL WITH HIGH CONFLICT FAMILY LAW CASES

"If We Manage Conflict Constructively, We Harness Its Energy for Creativity And Development"
- Kenneth Kaye

At Resolution Matters, our primary focus is working with clients who have experienced trauma in their family system. When parties decide that mediation is best, we can, and often will, employ a therapist who works with us in conducting the mediation. We often develop an interim agreement that addresses issues such as housing, seeing other people, and compensation if additional income is needed when the other spouse was the primary source of income. This is called pendente lite or pending litigation, which is achieved by negotiating a consensual agreement with the parties or petitioning the court for relief. The interim agreement gives the family members a degree of certainty for the short term while the legal process moves toward a final agreement.

The role of the parenting coach (trained psychotherapist) is critical in working with families experiencing high emotional intensity. It is usually in these situations that a collaborative law process may be best suited as having coaches at the table with the parties to ground and focus the conversation in a more constructive manner. This will always be the first option when family members have a high level of distrust and anger and do not want to even be in the same room as the other. From the trauma perspective, by not dealing with the issue, we have learned that certain negative scenarios could repeat themselves. Therefore by having trained mental health professionals working with us, we find there is a greater probability to transform these matters into something more constructive.

Other Solutions Before Litigating

When we first talk to a client, they share concerns that they are aware of and we identify other unknown concerns. It is necessary to have a professional guide them through this process. At Resolution Matters, we go through what is called the spectrum of possible methods of resolving their case during the initial interview process. We view possible methods along a continuum so that we explore various options with our clients. The client then decides how they would like to proceed legally.

If we look at the various resolution options from left to right, the left is the least invasive. It is called the kitchen-table model and is often the preferred method. It means that family members are comfortable enough to sit around the kitchen table to discuss and work out some, if not all, agreements. If there are few arguments, there will be less time devoted to negotiating. This creates a more efficient and cost-effective process.

The next process moving along the spectrum is facilitation. This is usually a simple process where my firm Resolution Matters and possibly another lawyer would facilitate the agreements among the family members. Counsel in this instance may provide an outline of the elements of a comprehensive settlement that gives the parties power of the terms of the agreement and potentially save attorney fees and costs.

After that on the spectrum is mediation. Mediation can take on various shapes and sizes. It can adapt to whatever the issues are. In the case of divorce, Resolution Matters lawyers work with both parties to agree on financials, parenting plans, and other separation issues. We might need to bring in experts from various fields to assist with the agreements at hand. Experts might include therapists, parenting coaches, economic experts, and financial advisors.

Moving more toward the center of the spectrum is the collaborative law model. At the heart of collaborative law, the process is the notion that all sides have individual representation of counsel. They sit down and collaborate, creating agreements to resolve their differences. They also agree that if the case does not settle, the lawyers will not continue into litigation.

One advantage of the collaborative process is that the parties can come to mutual agreements that might not have been an option in litigation. It can be done in such a way that balances the delicacy of the family fabric, especially where young children are involved. This can stop family members from experiencing recurring trauma.

The next process along the continuum is called arbitration. This is often confused with mediation, but arbitration requires a third party to make either a binding or non-binding decision on a particular issue. Often in a divorce, arbitration is used around custody, since arbitration is not done in public. The advantages are that arbitration is done outside the court, is expeditious, and is up to the parties involved to select the arbitrator who they think is equipped and has the skill level to respond to the issue in question.

From arbitration, we move to litigation. Litigation might be more appropriate in more serious situations, such as domestic violence. It is often a last resort or happens when the involved parties cannot be in the same room to work out an agreement. Lastly is full-blown litigation. It is our opinion that working in the earlier stages of the continuum is preferable. It often saves the client's time and money, while not exacerbating the client's prior trauma as litigation might do.

CHAPTER 11

PREPARING CLIENTS FOR NEGOTIATION

When heading into a negotiation, Attorney Shapiro spends time going over what is considered a successful negotiation. At Resolution Matters, we provide clients with seven elements to help heal any trauma experienced through this process. These elements give the clients a resource for coping with the process ahead of them. We do this by:

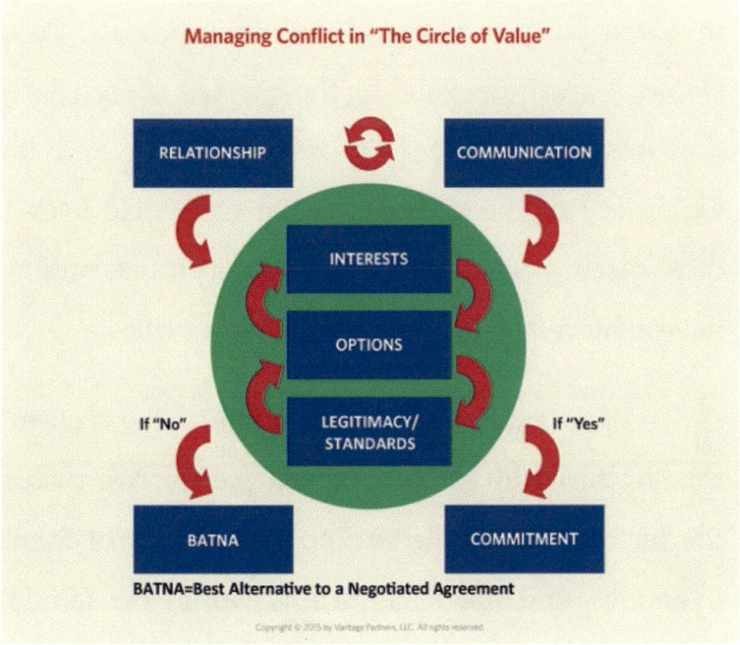

Exhibit: Managing Conflict in "The Circle of Value". Harvard Negotiation Project, Interest Based Negotiation and Getting to Yes, by Roger Fisher and William Ury.

The diagram above depicts three of the elements at the core of negotiations, with two elements at the top and two at the bottom of the circle. The inner three are what is needed/essential to get to an agreement (Yes), that should be the focus of each involved party throughout the entire process. Those elements are understanding the interests of each party, the possible options for a settlement, and the legitimacy of the settlement. We will circle back to these discussion areas throughout the process until we have achieved equilibrium in the settlement.

We start with discussing the client's relationship with other involved parties. We discuss the history of the relationship, the history of family dynamics, and the relationships within the family's community. We work with the client to ensure that they know that we will help them receive the full support needed while going through the legal process. They need to know that they are not alone.

Also at the top of the circle is communication. Communication is a key component to moving forward in a high-conflict situation. This is when we might use the balcony described earlier. The client will practice co-regulated breathing, where you practice breathing along with the person next to you in the situation. This helps the client to learn to communicate in a more thoughtful, constructive, and direct way. They find their voice and build courage.

At the bottom of the circle is commitment. The legal process does not happen automatically but takes time. The client must muster the strength and persistence, along with compassion for themselves to stay in the legal process. They understand that there is a possibility of being re-traumatized during the legal process, but they can work through it. The commitment also contemplates and budgets for this process resolution. If you commit to making the other party miserable you only going to make yourself miserable and spend more than necessary in the process. Whereas a commitment to working collaboratively with the professionals involved will assist in moving through the inertia that gets in the way of a settlement.

Lastly, at the bottom of the circle is the best alternative to a negotiated agreement. In this case, we are comparing whether settling the dispute out of court is better than going to court for litigation or not.

Then we move to the center of the circle, to the **interests** of the parties involved. At this stage, we really investigate and look at what is important to each party. We use our full resources in the most expansive way rather than compromise. The client begins to understand what is important to them.

The second element inside the circle is **options** for a settlement. This is where the brainstorming happens. The options might be rough drafts or lists. This gets the parties involved thinking about why they want certain items included or not included in the settlement.

The third element inside the circle is **legitimacy**. The agreement must meet the legal requirements of the state and other entities that might have some oversight of the final agreement.

Our team at Resolution Matters is committed to resolving your family dispute in the least disruptive and least costly manner.

What Is The Next Step?

For more information on Complex & Traumatic Family Law Cases, an initial consultation is your next best step. Get the information and legal answers you are seeking by calling (301) 795-2444 today.

INDEX

NOTES

Made in the USA
Monee, IL
05 November 2026

67387949R00057